UNEARTHING
IDA

Poems by
Rose M. Smith

GLASS LYRE PRESS

Copyright © 2019 Rose M. Smith
Paperback ISBN: 978-1-941783-63-4

All rights reserved: Except for the purpose of quoting brief passages for review, no part of this book may be reproduced or transmitted in any form or by any means, electronic or mechanical, including photocopying, recording, or by any information storage and retrieval system, without permission in writing from the publisher.

Design & Layout: Steven Asmussen
Cover Art: Christinlola | Dreamstime.com
Copyediting: Elizabeth Nichols

Glass Lyre Press, LLC
P.O. Box 2693
Glenview, IL 60025
www.GlassLyrePress.com

Praise for Unearthing Ida

In the poems of *Unearthing Ida*, Rose M. Smith reveals a cultural history and a personal history of an African American family and their Alabama roots. The remarkable thing here is that Smith allows these family members to speak for themselves, and those voices are very credible. The persona is a mask that reveals and Smith's use of the persona in this collection is stellar. A command of diction and syntax is used to create the character speech of Smith's powerful and beautiful archetypes. This is a created oral history put to music. The language is the gospel of the blues, and I was caught in the flow of it. I know this place, and I know these people because Rose M. Smith has made the introductions.

—**Gary Copeland Lilley**, author of *The Bushman's Medicine Show*

In imagining the life of a woman like her mother, Rose Smith casts light on the lives of many. This book recalls Rita Dove's *Thomas and Beulah* and, before it, Jean Toomer's *Cane*, achieving, like them, a resonance that moves well beyond the personal. In *Unearthing Ida*, Smith gives voice to 20th century Black women, military families, the mentally ill, children and the aged, and speaks plainly back to the routine abuses by men and the medical establishment against those they perceive as powerless. Line by line, these are poems that wound, that debride a wound, that prove how language holds for all of us a cleansing, healing space, should we wish to reach out and take it.

—**Kathy Fagan**, author of *Sycamore*

UNEARTHING
IDA

Foreword

Ida was born into a farming family in southern Alabama in the late 1920s, ninth of sixteen siblings, the quiet one you would not notice, most of her life spent observing the lives of others and waiting for her own. As she nears the limit of her years, she has become, to most, invisible.

Ida is not alone.

Acknowledgments

The author would like to thank the editors of the following publications in which some of these poems first appeared:

Dying Dahlia Review: "Unearthing Ida"
Halfway Down the Stairs: "Making Sweet"
Mom Egg Review: "Surrogates"
Not Dead Yet: An Anthology of Survivor Poetry: "One Night Fosters"
Passager, 2018 Poetry Prize honorable mention: "When a Country Steals Your Sons"
Snapdragon: A Journal of Art and Healing: "Conversations at the Manor"
Third Wednesday: "Labyrinth I", "Leave", "Morning, IV Time"

I am extremely grateful to the following people who assisted with this manuscript: Steve Abbott, Michael Block, Kathleen Burgess, Charlene Fix, Kwoya Fagan Maples, Rikki Santer, Bianca Spriggs. Thanks as well to those of you who encountered one or more of these poems in workshop or gifted me your time to provide a word, a comment, or a suggestion. You stoked the fire. You kept me going. You brought me joy.

To anyone who contributed in some way to this project and I failed to mention you, grant me grace. Forgive me, please. Forgive. It was a long journey from there to here.

Contents

Unearthing Ida — 1

Topsoil, Alabama

When a Country Steals Your Sons — 5
The Dailies — 6
Bussed — 7
Clap — 8
Meeting Howard — 9
First Morning — 10
Firsts — 11
New Dance — 12
A Thing for Flowers — 13
Buckshot Run — 14

Subsoil

Making Sweet — 19
Leave — 20
Labyrinth I — 22
Nights with Sister Annie — 24
Growing Good Crop — 25
Spider Song — 26
Processionals — 27
Pulse — 29
Interrupt — 32
Instructions for Staying — 33
Camarillo — 34
Different — 35

Subsoil (cont'd.)

Second Starts	36
Ida Moves to Buffalo	38
The Physics of Mentally Ill	39

Regolith

Home Visit	43
Longing For	44
Sojourn in Motown	45
Brotherly	47
Walnuts on the Ground	48
One-Night Fosters	49
Don't Say My Happy	51
Blood Ties	52
Hopelessly Romantic	53
Mother and I Sit for Hours in Her Front Room	54
Bow	55
The Creeping Numb	56
Stolen in the Break	59
The Crazy One	60
Meditations	62

Regolith (cont'd.)

Labyrinth II	63
Riverside	64
Conversations at the Manor	66
Surrogates	67
Meal Times at the Manor	69
Vigils	70
Sinai's Grace	71
Back	73
Morning, IV Time	74
The Visitor	76
To a Sound of Water	77
Choice	78
Afterword	81
About the Author	83

Unearthing Ida
Rosie, Sinai Grace Hospital, June 2014

Trained hands remove the fabric scrim
slowly, by turns, by shifts, reveal
valley of hip, sloped crag of empty
womb, uncover flesh

the color of desert sand,
landscape eroded to rift and waver,
stark, creased, rippling
where muscle once shaped the dunes.

Help me turn her, the aide requests.
We roll forward pelvic cradle, rib,
outcrop of shoulder, blade, every ridge
peeking through skin a history

written in this shell of once woman.
Ida holds her stroked right arm aloft
as we prop her weight
to let the bedsore breathe.

Morning nurse, blood pressure band,
reaches for the right.
Ida gargles words
behind her stroke-stolen tongue,
over and over, flailing.

Nurse croons an it's alright
at strange Ida noise,
pumps the cuff, assumes dementia.
She said use the left, we tell the nurse.
Pause: Surprise. Held breath. Apology.

TOPSOIL, ALABAMA

"... land offered a promise to future generations ... No matter what misfortune or oppression might come (short of God's wrath or drought and pestilence), the family could support itself ... and pass on that security to children and grandchildren."

— *"Black Farmers in America",* John Francis Ficara,
Juan Williams, NPR.org, February 22, 2005

When a Country Steals Your Sons
Ida's father, Eldridge, 1946

First you shake fists at God and sky
when Sam comes for your boys. Five times
you watch them board a bus, promise you
to write, one by one as days line up,
longer 'til the harvest. Just so many times
you make the heartbreak stiff your backbone up,
take it like medicine, bitter as yellowroot,
like Solomon's Seal when the absence rends
your bones, arms aching across desert and sea.
Some sons you don't get back, your feet alone
left to walk this land they loved.

What you can see from here, acres north
and south of old Route 1, are me and mine,
what we have, what we give, our blood
and sweat on every one. Up this road
the house raised also by hard work,
our hands that troweled every mortar line,
the lingering songs of Glory
that carried us through long days,
strong sons' hands at trough and plow
set alongside to help.

Fifteen times the waters broke, labor rent
new life from their mother's cries.
Now even though alive, these sons
rise to the commands of men who rally
at the call of oil, not the calling of the land.
Now even daughters smell the scent
of lives not written on this soil.

The Dailies
Ida, 1946

1.
Rise before the Leghorn crows
throw on clothes in the dark
first light best time to hit a row
half a dozen maybe
Pull the soft from open shell
seed and all

2.
Papa didn' raise no slack, no lazy girl,
no soft town-spoiled or useless frill.
Raised us smart. Gin-lever smart,
world-ready smart
enough to know the scent
of college boy blues and wannabes,
pockets full of old Sam's money.

3.
Sharp edges of the pod slice
tender fingers open
like the curled edge of a knife,
quick then red, snatch-back
reflex when you're not lookin'.
Best keep your head about you in the work.
Each bag a covenant signed early
with your father's hand.
Callouses an armor you wear proudly.
Each new day a harvest.

Bussed

Ida, 1947

Day Lena and I took the bus to Selma,
strange yellow streaked 'cross the sky
almost as if sun shone up from ground,
made us lean and stare as familiar lumbered by—
fields grown heavy with listening ears,
birds tellin' Papa we were coming back,
clouds gathering in a swift to pour
buckets over us, wake us from adventure.

Was no tellin' us anything, grown as we were
'cept maybe how long to the next quick station.
We stepped on quick, walked like prims
to the way-back seats. Good place
to watch strange faces getting on,
convince ourselves it was easy sneaking off.
Easy to pretend on the two-block walk
to the five-and-dime later that we belonged
in that new place where people lived
so close together. People milling on the street
'round storefront and other brick.

Boys from the base,
slim brown girls with oxford shoes,
hair greased up, curled short to their ears.
In the store window a sign said 6:00,
start time for The Hop we knew
Papa'd kill us for attending. But after
hours on a bus? We'd earned that night.
Nothing would send us running back
to corn fields, cotton, and Glory.
Even the reverend strolling up.
Well, maybe the reverend, but no one else.
We had rugs to cut soon as we could
figure out how.

Clap

Ida, 1947

Hattie Lee had a real mean hop step,
feet a quick blur doin' the 'bug,
swishin' her skirt like no way home.

Fast tunes like that, I'd take a wall,
cheer her on with a rock and a swing,
nobody changin' my side tune.

Nights like that we kicked awhile,
swingin' along in our country style.
Can't nobody own what you can't take back,
swift kick of rhythm, a clap and a jive.
Can't nobody own what you swing and slide,
swift kick of rhythm, a clap and a jive.

Meeting Howard

Ida, 1948

He calls me Beautiful. And there I am,
stranded on the tip of his tongue,
near that roomful of soldier boys
but waiting in a dim hallway.
And all I can think is frozen
in twenty years of not noticed,
of brothers calling me *skinny girl*.
Daddy's girl—not woman, not pretty,
just Ida. So I think to myself
it's the hair. It's always that *good* hair
quick boys all pulled and church friends
played with all through sermons, now
shiny black magnet for young men's fingers,
shimmering silk curled down my back.
Announcement of a tribe I do not know
but they say we also come from.
The hair, I think, and never for a minute
he sees ought else
in an olive-skinned girl
waiting for her dance-weary friend,
for her only ride home,
backside hugging the wall.

First Morning

Ida, Montgomery, 1949

Blindsided Howard looks next morning,
waking up to nice, warm me as if from a dream,
then pulls the sheets up like a girl,
swings his body from the bed.
His back to me, he clears his throat.
Ida? as though to the wall,
as though a grave mistake he's made,
then pulls on his shorts, rises
like shower steam from our bed.

Outside, a car slows, backfires
as it rumbles past. Somewhere
down the street a young boy calls his dog.
Across the hall, a woman's muffled laughter
and the soft moan of her lover,
heavy boots running toward the stair.
Howard turns to the bedside table,
barks, *Oh, shit!* at his watch,
yanks on his fatigues with a shuffle hop
then stares at my body as he buckles up.

Last night's promises hit the floor between us
as he grabs his shirt, turns away to button,
drops his arms, face lifted to the ceiling.
Duffle thrown to shoulder,
he huffs the space full of silent ghosts:
All the *how sweets, so beautifuls,*
so goddamn goods he'd moaned into my neck
when night and whiskey wrapped him
all around me.

Gotta go; I'll write; promise.
A quick sprint to the door.
Marriage paper left on the dresser.

Firsts

Ida's brother Albie, 1999

Ida was an A. Like A sharp. Like a slant chord thrown in at the right place, to change possibilities. No end to what she was liketa do. Like first letter of the alphabet, making way for others to follow. Not the first girl, first child, first much of anything, and just some chick, but first girl of Daddy's to walk away one day without askin'. First girl went off, got a job. Met some fly boy, got married overnight. Left overnight. Thought he'd be her ticket to fill her hunger for college books. Did not work out, though. Straight A's all the way 'til then did not mean tuition. All that smart just reason to brag, but a reason takes you nowhere 'less there's somewhere to go. And Howard—slick-legged talker—handed out hearsay, quiet whispers a few sweet words. Not two pennies to rub together didn't come from Uncle Sam but made that penny in his pocket sound like promises and pearls. Shipped straight off before the sheets got cold. But Ida didn't know Howard could not give her a thing. Not 'til she was left picking up her skirt. 'Til eight no-rent weeks later, takin' a slow bus home.

New Dance

Montgomery, 1949

Start again at the mustard seed
of hope a few days old, in utero, unknown
to the laugh-tensed muscle of your mother's joy,
the soft caress of her lover's calloused hand.

Begin with Two-Step and Lindy guided by
his quick hip glide, left arm warm on her back,
right hand broadcasting next move, next flip,
next spin before conversation dips to silence.

Begin with slow sax and bass, wily notes
that hypnotize them both into visions
of forever and meant-well vow.
Drink each peace of it like tall draft.

Smoothness like this—begin with this.
Let it run. Let it soften the sharp, cut
edge long before the last bite speaks
emptiness served up over china,
its light film sticky with time.

A Thing for Flowers

Khaki meets Ida, Montgomery, 1951

Soft skirt the yellow of dust on stamen
swingin' in a gentle breeze,
hair sleek, shiny, graceful neck thin,
she was pistil in the center of a gathered group,
all of 'em soft and gorgeous, but she,
she was life surrounded by almost,
by maybe, and a coupla sure things
whispered about. Untouched,
that's what it was drew me in.
Called to me like that.
Standin' at not quite sundown
on the boardwalk right outside
the general store. And Kit and Jimmie
nudged me, pushed me up on her
with sly elbows, sideways grins.
Olive skin pinked by an hour or so
standin' 'round in sun and August soup,
sweat glist'nin' on her upper lip
'n' I wouldn't have said a word
'til she looked dead at me,
eyes smilin', mouth a question.
That's what I tell 'em when they ask me
what I saw in that old mealy-mouthed girl,
standin' back on her heels,
arms 'cross her chest
like a school teacher waitin' for quiet
but determined not to yell.
So I just leaned in and, real gentle-like,
told her, *Hey, I can't much dance either.*
And there it was—smile a hint of secrets
hidden under all that farm girl glow.
No big sparks, no magic. Just a bit of a nod.
A daylily sheltered by a wall, barely
catchin' that swing, lookin' too sweet to pick.
But me with a thing for flowers.

BUCKSHOT RUN
Ida's brother Albie, 1999

Fool old tractor would not run that day,
else I would not have seen that fella come strolling
up. Starched crease of a uniform. Stiff-lipped hat.
Asked for Eldridge 'n I thought *Oh, no.*
Here we go again. Daddy bout t' run off
another shiny boot tryin t' cut a rug
with Flora. With Eldrina or some such.

I figured that was about to be a real short visit
'cause they'd both got on 'bout some school teacher
hired down the road and might as well
had on ankle irons for all the further they'd get
to go. Turns out this soldier fella was after Ida.
Storm on Daddy's face made his skin look gray.
Passed by quick, but dark. No surprise—
they say she was Daddy's favorite.
Ida weren't no queen. May be he thought
she'd always be right there,
Mama being sick like she was.

If you'd asked me then,   I   would   have
said,   *Five   minutes.   Five minutes*
'fore soldier boy'd come runnin' out quick.
Daddy been known to send a fella or two
on a buckshot run asked the wrong thing
'round there. But this fella?
(*Khaki,* she called him later.) This fella
took up on the couch 'cross from Daddy
nearly two hours just talking. Stayed for dinner.
Walked 'round to the back and down
along the pasture still holding his hat.
And   came   back   alive.
Shook hands on his way out.

Knew right then weren't no sense thinking
nothing else but Ida gone. Daddy…
he didn' let nar' one of his girls
touch a toe out past where he gave his
permission. Permission or strap.
One or the other.

Wish I'd known right then Khaki wadn' no count.
Yes, sir. Wish I'd known right then.

Subsoil

"Many people with serious mental illness are challenged doubly. On one hand, they struggle with the symptoms and disabilities that result from the disease. On the other, they are challenged by the stereotypes and prejudice that result from misconceptions about mental illness. As a result of both, people with mental illness are robbed of the opportunities that define a quality life: good jobs, safe housing, satisfactory health care, and affiliation with a diverse group of people."

—*Understanding the impact of stigma on people with mental illness*, Patrick W. Corrigan and Amy C. Watson, *World Psychiatry*, February 2002

MAKING SWEET

Ida, Montgomery, 1952

Oil from the rind sticks, bitter
on your fingertips, tacky reminder
you worked that yellow fruit
down to broken pulp,

a circular rendering
deep into the core,
a slow hard squeeze,

every drop of life
pressed from its ragged pulp.

Lemon for codfish,
lemon for your pekoe black,
plural for your iced –ade
after you pour in

more sugar than the drip deserves.
To make the sweet sweet,
make the heaven heaven.

Then quite by accident
you lick the acrid tips,
discover new contortions
of lip and face, soured
reminder not everything is
as it seems.

Leave

Ida, Montgomery, 1953

Starched khaki uniform shirt he was,
three stripes proud and three sheets
into base-leave wind. He was red goatee.
He was Benjamin's buddy—short but not too
short rib for starving body. He was rib.
He was hard bone, warm breath,
breath. He was ticket. Ticket out.
Ticket off. Ticket away from.
Freak, foolish, fearful, forsaken.
Farm.   Father.
Starched Khaki—swing dance
straight-toothed ticket to forgetting.

A *forget* for the remembering

For forgetting
first-husband-tossed blood words
scabbing on open ear.
Starched Khaki was ear sugar,
wet lash, seeking tongue,
long night in town promise.
He was promise—whisper
into muffle, caution, muffle,
one-handed whirl, two-step
swaying narrow hip,
nudge, coax, lever, push,
sweet berry sling-back thrust.
He was thrust, trust siphoned up
from backward farm girl thrush,
rush, peacock prance, slick
seeding magic come—and,
command, command, come
and go.

A remember for all the *forget.*

He was   *remember.*   He was
burn. Red poker soul brand burn, like Daddy
warned you 'way from burn. God damned
good for nothin', *Girl, you married* burn,
eclipsing old darks. He was sun.
Body lighting, life giving, free....

Muster.

He was phone.
He was phone call, postcard, absence,
stunned-silent hard life rule breaker sun,
babe-bringing sun, dark ordinary
in Saudi sun hero suit son.
Gone sun. Cloud-heavy sun.
Everyday rain sun. Not rain.
Behind the rain. Behind dark sky,
behind cry, behind wait. He was
wait. He was cross-legged, end swell,
shameless beg wait, another phone
call, post card, wait, no-money wait,
body-hungry wait, storm-on-horizon
wait, never returning. Turning me....

Labyrinth I

Ida's alternate self speaks of 1954

When first I sheltered Ida, at Autauga,
her thin fingers had worn to fray
the hem of a spring-yellow blouse
as her belly pressed in all morning.
Seat of her skirt soaked from the amnion,
I felt her heart go double time,
peered through to find her frozen, fear
raging through every room within us both.
The hard vise of her practiced body
cinched forward toward the birth while Ida
cowered in the labyrinth's far corner.

It was I who moved her to the door,
told her sister, mother it was time.
I lay her on the mat, urged her to wake
as her sister kneaded low back muscle,
prayed Ida'd feel the love in those strong hands,
but her tremble shook the labyrinth walls,
made thunder as she crouched,
filling her corner with whispers.

I had them send for Sister Annie
to wife her through the flood,
breathed for Ida in cleansing repetitions
as her heart echoed like *djembe* drumbeats
off the walls she'd raised.
How had she conjured such a pattern?
Even I could walk that labyrinth for days
and never find the door.

As the babe crowned, Ida woke
to Sister Annie's ministrations,
felt steel jaws close around her life.
It was I who pushed the down head free,
I who forced the bastard shoulder into waiting hands
while Ida cowered, afraid she'd see a stranger
in the new babe's face.

I stretched her hands forward
to receive the bawling girl,
whispered, *See, Ida?*
This is not the face of your transgression.
No one will ever know.

When Khaki claimed the new child
was not his, I held Ida's quaking shoulders
still for days, guided the babe to her breast,
sang to her of spiders, water spouts and rain
'til the babe's sweet gurgle reined her into mothering.
I am still here now.

I am still here.

Nights with Sister Annie

When lights up the hill are distant stars
in a cool gone-ebony night, you need
the practiced hand of conjure woman,
nightingale. Annie comes in a wisp,
her eyes beacons to call your wellness home.
Her gentling cloths laid across your brow
ease muscle untrained at laboring
new life into tomorrows uncharted,
infinitesimal, open.

Base doctors in lab coats will not happen
toward this place. No embrace of numbness
offered—not by needle or by mask.
Instinct draws an inner grid,
pulls its edges like a drawstring
over swollen belly, whispered fears,
aloneness stark as white birch trunks
on hillsides during rain, each one a sign
of long endurance. Your child's cries echo
over corn and weed, her eyes clenched
tight against her life's bright glare.

Growing Good Crop

Ida's sister Flora, Alabama, 1959

Don't let 'em see the signs,
Colored Only entrance markers
on property not family-owned.
How good it is to have
your blood's own place
to take your feet, buy your goods,
sell extra from your own fields,
full of generations.

Take them through safe places—
the general store where open hands
lift them high, where memories that linger
smell like family fruit, bolts of cotton
fabric waiting to be made dresses.
Where favorite images long past now
will taste like coconut bars picked
from big glass jars on the counter
and cousins who bent to smile and take
their prized two-penny payments.
Where no one made them feel like less.

Keep them from spit, from stares,
from insults thrown at their young skins, insults
tossed harder than any strap with its tearing burn.
Nothing like holding life accountable
for the shape young girls' minds take.
Let no one brand them prisoner or peasant,
nigra, dark one, servant before they know
what they can be.

Spider Song

Ida, at Khaki's mother's home, Ohio, 1959

Her head in my lap, I squeeze
pinkeye ointment into held-wide eyes,
tell her, *Hold them closed until I say,*
watch her flutter beneath anxious lids
imagine she sees the tortoise shell brush
she pulls through my hair, love in every tug,
the smooth face of the pink satin ribbon
she pets with her pointer for comfort,
or our fingers in window sunlight
while we sing together *the itsy bitsy spider
went up the water spout,* her questions
ringing from these eggshell walls.

She'll be better here—grandmother hands
to hold and mold her, stable house
where she can blossom and become.
I've fought back the voices but still battle
rape shadow, side street, dark hallway,
each door from which his face might spring,
knife blade pressed to my neck.
Echoes in my head no longer silent,
bus ticket hidden in my purse.

I am the spider.
Down comes the rain.
You can open now.

Processionals

Ida, at Camarillo, thinks of Khaki, 1961

Tell me again the meaning of promise made
in the presence of a sea—friends' faces
seated in celebratory lines, golden rings
as special as the price we paid

for what might last forever. Tell me
how big the reverend smiled, how beautiful
we all looked that day just before the rain
cut short a fine reception.

Was told my fear of water after I was grown.
Still do not swim; but climb I can, fingers rough
from hanging on, feet accustomed to small fissures,
to edge forward toward light. This journey I trained for:

How to make good biscuits, cut 'em with a tin cup—
nice, round and even. How to rise up early, sizzle
fatback, eggs, and summer squash before day begins
and hold back the rush of words when storms come.

How to cradle babes, soothe 'em, press away letdown
'til the dinner's done, treasure the weight
of old memories hanging from this tired blind
in a tiny upper flat. The thick wet heat of seasons.

Now no 'Bama breeze, no acres and no you.
Do not whisper your sorry.
This three-cord strand broke long before
that postcard from active duty—

*no knowledge of this woman who says
that child is mine.*

True bottom is mercy weather, flooding gullies,
old truck sliding off muddy Route 1.
Mark an 'x' on a safe spot high above me;
move aside and let the red hills shade my face,

point the path through these spectators
lined to watch our fretful film.
Heavy-line the route away from this.
Show me the direction out.

Pulse

Ida on ECT[1], 1961

Woke up nowhere, reaching for my why.
Gray-haired Sally purring. *Time to take your pills.*
Remembered card game in the common room,
someone beating tables, loud drumbeat
like boots marching unison. Yes.
Boots. Marching. Starched Khaki. Music.
That voice again in my head.
Worthless, you hear me? Worthless.

So I ask Sally did she hear that. She
calls the doctor every time.
Doctor so sexy I think I want him,
but this man steals memories.
Old sexy white-man croon, *Quiet, Ida,
or we'll have to do a treatment.
Do you want another treatment? Hmmm?
Is that what you need, Ida?* Then something
mumbled to two more blue-shirts.
Lighter blue. Not EMT blue.
Oh, God-not-again blue.
Coming-again-to-steal-me blue.

So, I practice:

> You had a child in Montgomery, Ida. She stilled
> 'neath your waist when the dam broke, slid out
> singing in a place like this—white uniform
> and bassinet, apgar score and scream.

1: *Electroconvulsive Therapy (ECT) was a common treatment for various mental illnesses in the 1950s and early 60s, especially schizophrenia. Up to 80% of ECT patients experienced some form of amnesia, losing either the hours leading up to treatment or weeks or years prior to the event.*

Your sister's nose, your father's eyes,
mother's long-suffering tow.
Feet in rack, shots in your back,
sleep between contractions, you had her, held her.
Thin and sweet, little puckered lips.
Remember, Ida. Remember.

You had a child in Autauga on a mat of blankets
in your father's house, your mother's room.
Canal marauder, bowed legs waving, she came.
No rack, no anesthetic quilt, she came.
Squatting like a break in the fields 'til she came.
Lifted into Sister Annie's hands. She wears
your nose, your eyes, your jumpy little fidget
and a smile. Round cherub face, Ida. Remember.

Grip the fragile thread, Ida. Think.
Grip. Think. Remember. Tuck.
Tuck them away before the pulse:
Two kids, backyard, chickens, pasture on a hill,
trees back by the fence, gate to the garden,
summer cukes, summer corn, summer squash.
Squash them deep into that brain
of yours. Tuck, Ida, tuck. Cover them
before they take you. Cover the back home
things, the light. Cover the love-sweet things.
Cover sweet child, checked dress, photos,
Sundays at Glory Baptist, kids in tow, baby brother's
smile. Pull them back from the keening ledge.

Say, *It'll all be alright tomorrow*
Say, *Little brother, don't run. Stay.*

Say, *Hold on. Don't let go.*
Say, *Cling to the wet with me.*
Hold the synapse tight, grit your teeth.
You are stronger than pulse, than membrane. Hold.
Think, *I had a daughter. No, two.*
Think sister, father, farm, freedom, alone.
Think, *Alone.* No. Don't think alone.
Think, *Nobody knows the trouble I seen.*
No. Think, *No trouble.* Think, *No trouble.*
Think music and swing dance, Ida.
Think Doris on the tube. Think
dance at the air base, sweet Lena
skipping with you on red dirt road.
And no voices. Think no voices.
No voices. Think, *No voices.*
Think.... Think.... Think...

Gray-haired Sally leaning over me:
It's time to take your pills.

INTERRUPT
Ida's daughter Regina, Riverside, 1960

He showed up in Air Force green, hat like a paper boat tipped over on his head. And he was dark—darker than I remembered, darker than that picture Mama used to hold, but Daddy anyway. Standing in the big gym doorway while we practiced the new spring play. I was picked to sing, had lines to speak, pale pink princess dress with gold ricrac on the edges, all ready for the show. When they called us down from that little stage, oxfords shushing on the scuffed wood floor, we thought it was for hello, to welcome the family mystery home. Then home became a bus, stopping here and there for days. Then home was this upstairs bedroom, hot, sticky air blowing in through thin white curtains. Rocket ship radios. Dolls with skin like Mama's coffee. This man trying hard to buy a place inside us. Inside us instead of in a picture. Trying to show us he could be what a daddy means.

Instructions for Staying
Ida thinks of Khaki, Riverside, 1961

Hold your peace. The old church women say
hold your peace as if they know what it's like
when he bares his teeth, growls
his hard commands, lets go
his rage at you without warning.

Hold your peace, I say to me.
Find your still-strong after
the mouth for which you hungered
spits ridicule, the hand and touch
you cherished lash out to cower you.

Hold your peace, they say
as Mama's eyes stare back at me
from the distance, admonish me
long years after she waved goodbye
from her funerary march.

Easy to say, these platitudes.
Not one back of her man's hands
tossed hard truths harder. Still
she whispers her wisdoms
right from the grave, soft words to my
listening-daughter eyes, excuses
for a swift-armed errant son.

CAMARILLO

Ida, California, 1961

You lose the years in that place, lose track of where you are, what time, what day, lose your self.   Lose what you'd wanted to be, the you you studied to be. That you everybody called so smart, called scholar, said would go so far. You measure day from wake to bedtime, by meds in the cup, mealtime, recreation room, bath time, and long talks with white coats when you don't know what to say, how to say, when, why. You measure time by letters from family, promised visits never made. School pictures of children you remember, children you do not know. Only you're happy they can't see you, don't want them to see you.   *Not like this.*

Different

Regina, Ohio, 1962

She came back different, I think. Not different to see, but different like not Mama. Different like someone who used to talk but doesn't anymore. Nothing but *C'mon* when it's bath time or a hand waving us off to bed, long fingers hanging like Catalpa pods you pick up from the ground. Nothing but *Y'all, come eat,* to get us to breakfast. *Come eat,* dinner to dinner every night. She said those things perfectly. She brushed our hair, pulled clean clothes from the dresser drawer, helped Rosie tie her shoes. But different. No music anymore, no afternoon TV. No little songs, no jazz-on-the-radio solo dance we used to giggle to, no sideways winks, finger to her lips after secrets. No more finger games, Old Maid at the table. Doll house not filling up with tiny treasures. And we missed the patty cake and Mary Mack, shadow puppets on the wall, the M, I, crooked letter, crooked letter, I, crooked letter, crooked letter, I, humpback, humpback, take it all back, humpback humpback I. Some things you can't get back.

Second Starts
Ida to her sister Flora, 1964

Felt silly as a twelve-year-old
comin' back to Daddy's house after
gettin' married and all that. Twice.
After all that time at Camarillo.
After Khaki signed me in, took the Fairlane
and the kids, took what little joy I'd wrung
out of that tiny upper flat—only
cold water and his disagreeable ass.
'Rillo let me out, though, so here I am.

Every time I turn into the East bedroom,
I expect to find you and Melvin
all caught up in each other's faces like the old days.
You're not here, but you're here.
Hope you understand this.

Even harder turning into Mama and Daddy's room
with Old Witch on my mind. Still can't believe
he asked that woman to marry him.
She was widowed. He was widowed.
He was lonely, I guess. That's Daddy.
After all, there *are* sixteen of *us*.
Old Witch only shows up every week or two,
like the only time she needs to be with him is
when she needs to *be* with him. Then
she goes back to her own place.
So I do the wash, make Daddy's bed,
and cook.
He eats it alright.

Dusted the floor and the furniture in his room:
He's got a picture of Old Witch sitting in there

I near' pretended it fell and broke it.
She is *uuuugly*. Can't shake the walls—
it's a sturdy house
but she sho could break a mirror. Bitch.
(Sorry.) Last thing this house needs is her
hovering 'round Daddy like money
gon' find its way from somewhere buried
straight into her purse. That's all she wants.
She figures she can let 'im have a little o' her
if she'll get all his land. And the house.
But if she moves in, where do I go?

Nobody hires schizos.
Not even Mr. Reggs at the store in town.
Tried. Once word gets 'round,
it's like having *crazy* stamped on your face.
But Daddy stacked these bricks.
He and Uncle Koerner raised
that barn and fence. Mama
made every meal on that old wood-burner,
every canned jar of carrots.
I bet Old Witch'd burn water.
Had the nerve to roll her eyes at me
when I set Daddy's place last Sunday.
Like I should o' had her plate ready, too.

Not in this house, not from this stove,
not by these hands. She sat right there
on her backside, watched me cook
the whole damn thing. She can go to hell
'fore I'll wait on her old mean ass.
House oughta reach right out and bite 'er
next time.

Ida Moves to Buffalo

Someone's turn to take the relic in,
the semblance of once-Ida wringing
hands in her lap, eyes lost in a now
of New York dim, in rote repetition:
Low risk task, low risk task,
low risk task. Risk, separation, retreat.

Someone's turn to make space,
feed the empty mouth that's left,
your children her children,
your empty room her room.
They'll take comfort from her quiet,
peace from her slow hand, from her.

There is a balm in this watching—
watching the woman watch
the child watch the woman,
mutual, guileless exchange,
woman cutting the crust from noontime,
serving life up in small bites to tiny hands.

The Physics of Mentally Ill
Ida, Buffalo, 1967

When she says how beautifully I made her
house perk up and shine like no "girl" had
before, I think of formulas: Velocity,
momentum, torque, acceleration,
where might I go if.

As she prattles welcome, upcoming plans,
my job long as I want, gives me
keys to servant quarters, I think
density, pressure, viscosity,
the Bernoulli effect on stagnant air
when doors open.

When these hands don't listen
and lethargy takes presence on my brain,
she says I daydream too much, move too slowly
getting all her things done. I think gravity,
weight, inertia, the arc of a pendulum
constant in tomorrow, my vision turned inward,
life no longer elastic again, again, again.

Regolith

"And I don't want the world to see me
'Cause I don't think that they'd understand
When everything's made to be broken
I just want you to know who I am"

—*Iris*, John Rzeznik for Goo Goo Dolls,
Dizzy Up the Girl, Warner Brothers, 1998

Home Visit

Regina, Ohio, 1967

She left us is all I need to remember, left us passed about from hand to hand. Didn't write letters, never called, then showed up one year on a bus. For a visit she didn't want to make. I was, what, maybe twelve years old, but I heard. Big Mama telling Pop Pop the letter came, someone else asking can Ida come to stay. And *Course!* would be Big Mama's answer. Naturally. Opening up her great big arms to soothe the broken hearts of all her sons' misfortunes. *Just for a week,* she said. A stranger in the front room, watching us. Then left again 'til high school graduation. Rosie doesn't remember that. Doesn't remember the years between, the pass-arounds.

All the empty space is mine.

Longing For

Ida, 1969

Now when the body remembers, it thinks
      muscle, lean, quiver-laden, full,
           of rushing blood,
                  finger tip and haunch,
           of pulse and beckon
                  pinking unscarred cheeks
                        spotted with sweat,

folds itself, thick, warmed by firewood
      or stones and begs
           to sooth the swell we once welcomed
                before we slept
                      cocooned.

This aching skin
      knows the rough of thick hands, hard
           from tool and labor, knows
                cool surface of pillow,
                  place,
                        recline.

The body stretches its internal hands
      toward a swift deluge of
           hungry homing in.

The body has a mind.
The mind is not my own.

Sojourn in Motown
15-Sibling Homelessness, Ida, Detroit, 1978

There is always a room when siblings share
the burden of you among themselves
for love or obligation. You don't think about
whether it's one or the other.
You go where they tell you, move
into whatever room they point you toward,
suitcase in hand, a few boxed clothes
carried by a nephew.

Everyone in such a hurry
makes my hands seem slow.
They talk at and not to you,
don't wait for you to answer before next
flurries of words, think you're addled
when your tongue waits for your command.
If I could sass like my sisters,
I'd be different already.

I remember hospital, townhouse, hospital,
farm, hospital, life an orbit set around
a paranoid sun. Someone always out to hurt,
someone always whispering you can't
in your ear, the drugs they say will help,
but you're not you when you are the you on drug.
I calculate sine, cosine, algorithms in this head,

my brain three steps ahead of you and wrestling
to respond in a way you'll understand.
But you move so fast I can't decide how to meet

your questions in not-me language,
or which of me will answer when the moment calls.

One moment after another.
Even while the world whirls too fast for you
to earn your way, there is a room.
There is always room.

Brotherly

Oddly quiet these words
the men around her speak.
She feels each one like hammer,
like vise, like steel arms restraining
while she chats with this gentle man,
impressive in his height, his confidence.
They run blocking patterns imposed
between solace and opportunity.
Quiet, yet as if to say,
She is ours and lonely;
you cannot have her.
As if to say, *You cannot take advantage.*

It offends, this thought that lonely
makes a full life shed its skin, fall away
on words passed in necessity between two
strangers pressed together into service.
Inside her, questions flutter like grounded fish,
aware of a death more intimate
as each gill sac implodes.
A confluence of well-meant protections,
she sees the desperation others have long written
like coded messages in calligraphy on her face.

Walnuts on the Ground
Rosie, Ohio, 2004

In '88 the uncles sold off dozens
of hard worked acres from the family farm.
Peddled them out to home builders primed
for a buck, maybe for many, did not bid
them sift through autumn quiet for the fall
of walnuts from dark, forgotten branches.
Heirs no longer children had played
in the aging trees' fruit-scattered pastures,
pelted each other's backs with the hardened hulls.
Heirs, oblivious to the seed inside.

What sale could not close as quickly as a well-oiled hinge
they deeded in small portions to those of us who'd sprung
from womb and loin—so many sons, sons' sons, daughters
with red dust on our hands. Mother called us owners
as we watched her once-lithe hands tremble
over cornbread, thick smoked ham and greens,
her knuckles sharp and prominent,
high neck tilted forward. We could not see
the scars where her lover-stranger's words
cut her years ago—so slightly open in the flesh,
so deeply open in heart she'd take a lifetime
to fold new skin over that raw edge
and still not recover.

Stockholm syndrome, they call the way the broken
hold helplessly onto love unspoken, first offenses
so much like this hardwood fruit, fresh-fallen.
How at just-right ripe the soft hull pulls away from
nat-ribbed shell, its inner hardness born to hold secrets inside.
How a short blade laid against a vein to bleed away forevers,
layers them over in decades of retreat—your long, loud scream,
the rough scrub of excuses,
until the shell breaks.

One-Night Fosters
Rosie remembers California, 1991

Everything in the Riverside chapter is the dingy white
of eggshells two half-flights up in an off-base military flat,
Regina and me lying in bed in the streetlight pall, scanning
faraway stations on rocket-ship-shaped radios

tryin' to drown out Daddy's *worthless* and *send you back*s
and Momma's muffled *don't want to*s, our curtains waving
change in on summer California breeze, breaking our happy
all the way to hell as I give up and fight for sleep.

Over my head, I hear music in the air...

That chorus I'd just memorized plays in louder than out-
of-range station static; and I see folding chairs on a concrete drive,
a little blond woman with puffy hair pacing 'tween rows
of folding chairs, leather book swinging, trying to sing

Jesus into slap-happy Air Force kids who'd come to her
driveway vacation Bible school every day for two weeks.
She served pretzels, cookies, chocolate milk and
something to do an hour a day in old hot Boringland.

Didn't hear music but took her word for it,
cut my story book cutouts, glued baby Moses
to his basket, floated him downriver, into
those famous rushes and some handmaiden's waiting hands

the way we find ourselves shuttled off the next day into
strange beds for the night while Daddy goes off, unexplained,
Momma in tow. No goodbyes, no explanations, just PJs
and a dark room, *Green Onions* playing from beyond the door.

Over my head, I hear music in the air...

Think I'm dreaming, really, when the door swings wide,
Dark and Scary walks toward me with a stagger, says,
Here. Take this. Something smooth, warm, mostly round,
a soft ridge wrapping round it, and a soft dip at the center.

You want to see your daddy again? Put this in your mouth.
Me eight years old, oblivious to anything that could mean,
I touch it again and think I've no idea where *here* is and
heck if I'm gonna stay someplace with little hard beds,

mean ol' kids who whined about movin' their room and
prob'ly will get us back for that when no one's looking.
Do it, comes that voice, *or you'll never see your momma
or your daddy again,* as my eyes adjust slowly to the light.

This is not pretzels, cookies or chocolate anything, but
I sure as heck ain't stayin' in this strange dark place.
So I lean in, and 'Gina's voice is not like 'Gina from 'cross the room,
says, *No! Don't do it, Rosie,* as the door opens again

and some woman's pulling Dark and Scary struggling
from the room, leaving me confused. There's hell to pay
from the sound of things out in the hallway, that woman
slapping Dark And Scary 'round with newspaper or a paddle

and Regina out of bed peeking out at them before she shuts the door.
If he does that again you bite him. She crawls back into bed.
We listen as the slapping stops and Dark and Scary's voice
moves off into the distance, back to bein' Daddy's Air Force friend.

Over my head, I hear music in the air.
There must be a God somewhere.

Don't Say My Happy
Ida, Detroit, 1989

Eddie coaxes hymns from the old piano
as we remember him a skinny kid running
circles around siblings and cousins,
their wizened smiles, their laughter
the tease of a rich life already reserved.

Mina pulls the brush through gently,
"braids" my hair as I recall my little girls'
hands and watch instead these
little joys in canvas shoes and plaids,
their bottoms dusting the hardwood floor.

Don't say my happy died in Riverside,
on a long train ride to Motown,
or on a bus ticket from Alabama
with the kids both gone. Happy lives
in a quiet room, free to walk away,

lives here, tucked under a mattress,
between pages of a black King James,
the gilt of its leaves worn away
by the brush of seeking fingers,
and counts a promise in each day not spent

among the broken. Happy is a rough stone
wall retaining memories lest they slough away
with each new passing storm. It is cold
against my cheek, scratchy, abrasive
keeping me constant and awake.

Blood Ties

Rosie, 2004

Mother's eyes list reasons we should all know
demons exist. The green they bleed, the foul grin
of temperaments shaped in bowels of a darkness
that insists where evil dwells. In her eyes, ancient theater
tragedy masks, horrible back-echoed laugh descending
into childhood dreams repeated for many years.

Sweat-wet waking forehead confirms my fear
that genes she'd laid beneath my skin would hatch
their swarm of evils, steal me, too.
At six years old, I heard her cry aloud to still their voices.
Had no idea what that strangled sound meant.
By my window at evening, cicada song constant in my ears,

night light pushing shadows back, cold hand of legacy
an insomnia sweeping me toward nothingness,
face to face again with the promise of her insanity,
I wonder where my end will take me. Will the world recall
my voice pealed out across the waves when I go absent?
Will I know that I have left here when I'm gone?

Hopelessly Romantic
Rosie, 2008

I can think of it like this if I want to:
She in a pale yellow summer dress,
he in fresh fatigues.
She, half-listening to giggling friends and
chattering to his young, smooth face.
She is saying only half as much
as soft streams running by red-dirt roads
after sudden storm.
Her black hair glistens
in the light of the dinner club
where Flora took her to shake off sadness
that hung from her like a drape.
I watch him touch her hand, feel him
tug her, watch them two-step
into my history book
on the edge of a cheap gold ring.
Most days I remember raised voices,
dishes, insults thrown, sleepless
nights she tossed about in visions—
his sun-browned arms wrapping the waist
of some town girl just miles from the post
he clerked for over two years in the war.
When all muddies into L.A. torrents,
I grant myself authority
to think of it like this when I want to:
They danced together beneath the moon,
two lithe bodies in a jazz-filled room
at least that once,
and I made all this difference.

Mother and I Sit for Hours in Her Front Room

Rosie, 2009

Few words split silence between these hungry souls.
Between cubes of summer sausage and cheddar taken easily
by two who know dinner already waits outside
for invitation to the table. Our history, this meal
before the meal. Waiting to be savored. Life with its leeks,
full flavored. Hard work to digest this stringy flesh.

We share a saucerful with wafers.
In the art of chewing party food, we can prolong
the anxious wait for layers peeled by years to season
the main attractions at family table, bring out
character, make tender
the years apart that made us strangers.

Her shoulders curl forward, arms sit cradled
in the lap grown small beneath post-middle-age
protrusions. Chin searches a place to rest where
clavicles clink together. A soundless percussion.
Even the body knows to shelter this
fragile heart. With time, the words come.

I have read of laboratories, lobotomies, controlling drugs,
shock treatments. Permanent rearrangement.
She describes her normalcy—Monday group therapy,
private consultations each four weeks. How she is
learning to be angry, fill the empty place, breathe
a self that feels and matters.

Grandchildren's exploits tug a smile from the sides
of her full lips. Her hands tremble over the cheddar plate.
Sudden motions come in waves as her neurons fire, random,
search for receptors burned away by therapy.
We nod agreement like schoolgirls sharing secret loves.
She admits there may be reason Father said I was not his.

Bow

Ida, about Riverside, 1999

Never told the girls 'bout leavin'.
Just disappeared with all my scars
and pains, pulled a wishbone
from the breast of broken promises.
Told myself not to leave them
crying ever again.

Letting go's not so hard.
Just open your hand, your heart,
let your mind think nothing's more
important than what you know:
A mother won't bow.
A mother won't know how.

She'll tuck all she's worth
beneath a borrowed mattress, hold it
'til some day brings her girls back
to her. She'll reach into her legacy
and give whatever's left as though
it is a priceless prize.

As though it can replace
the absence of her hands.

The Creeping Numb
the lingering fear of "or else," (of returning to psychiatric care)
Detroit, 2010

Tuesday. Ida.

First the right tongue gone slave to left,
its crisp tastes mottled, muddied. Forced
to push the soft spoonful to still-live buds,
salivary, speaking. Then right lip, lazy too,
its country curl, cynic half snarl, easy smile
buried in a growing fear of poison.
Then middle finger's slow bend inward,
the long ring next as if so tied, unmovable
as though pasted by third-graders' hands,
right arm weighted by imaginary harms.

Thursday. Ida

Run. The voice says, *Run.*
I say *poison*, to Dee's great hurt,
You tryin'a poison me. Then
board bus to a precinct bench, decry this
slow murder to men not listening
and wait.   Wait.   Even more wait.
At the day's first hour, in Dee comes,
sees a fool, untrusting aunt
cowering on polished pine.
It is her or the medics, her "or...."
I have seen *or* before.

Sunday. Ida.

Regina comes for me and all
my things when Dee calls.
At daughter's house, the leg
not right—its drunk response,
its dead skin shuffing against soft
pants. I am still already dead and will not eat,
reach for the phone to call the precinct
lest they all forget. Dee can't get away
with this. She can't get away with
this. Dee can't get away with this.
Then daughter calls the *or*.

Sunday. Regina to Rosie.

I had no idea what else to do. Dee calls, says, *You gon' have to come get your mother.* So I go. What was I going to do? Last week, Mama accused her of poison. Took a bus to the police station, told them Dee was trying to kill her. Police showed up at the house, Dee told them Mama's sick, and they sent her home. Now she won't drink anything. Won't eat. Won't take her pills. So I go get her. She was fine for a few hours, but still won't take her meds because "Dee poisoned them." Won't eat unless she makes it herself or watches me. Keeps trying to dial 911. I've had to hide the phones. Dr. Moore says bring her in; she needs to be admitted. I feel bad, Rosie. It feels so mean, but it's really all I can do. It's all I can do.

Wednesday. Ida's alter speaks.

She reached me in the or.
Stroke, they say, a slow onset
they would have missed, not for the or.
A slow onset they would have found,
not for the paranoid, the dread disease,
hiding its truth behind imagined threat,
keeping reason away. Keeping me
gone, too. I did not hear her, felt only
the going. A slow, incessant going
'til she called me in the or.

Stolen in the Break

Ida, after stroke, 2010

My open, my warm, my breath, my blood,
my silk slick flowing from hidden, my breach,
my breech, my life. My day breath crushed,
my night sweat fresh. All of these broken.

My hook, my gain, my shimmer, my scale,
my lost left, my straight back—gutted,
trophied on ingrained walls—my hurtless,
my marked edge, failed fret, toppled fence.
My can. All of these dos undone.

My half light, my guide, my ripped wrap, my whole,
my excised scar, covered head, side-glance eye.
My eye. My eye. My swollen. My crimped tongue,
swallow throat, sewn-shut scream. My right.
My walk. My strong walk home. My strong.
My private, my song. My war.

The Crazy One
Rosie, 2010

Mama danced upon the bed, waking us
late one Sunday in the summer,
right arm stretched to chandelier,
head flung back, a chanteuse belting out *I can*
to answer all the voices in her head.
I can touch the light. I can touch the light,
she declared while the voices cried back, *No.*
We laughed our little girl laughs,
heads buried under the sheets,
while we shouted,
Mama, don't dance.

Grown folks sent her to asylums to be fixed—
this woman, broken, strange,
not fit for mending children—
and there you have it:
two children, small and spindly,
passed from home to home,
tumblers in a lottery machine
to see who next would win
the mother prize.

Today we stand beside her angled bed,
pull her tray table forward.
We watch her grip the quaking fork—
bicycle handle bar—lift her eager feast,
leave gravy and potatoes on her cheek.
She tires with each lift, says her I can't,
struggles with this chewing—so hard now
what once was instinct, now foreign
movements she must master with this left.

The arm of declaration lies beneath her,
limp snake, head severed by a clot
no one could see as it came on slowly,
much like those voices years ago,
louder each day, but shared by no one,
a private reality no sane soul near her
could believe.

I pull the limp wrist from beneath her,
place it, lifeless on her belly.
Inside, I long for chandeliers in this sterile space,
want back the "crazy" one who ran from voices,
wailed of murder plots in late-night station houses.

Ida, two daughters standing here beside you
are your mother prize.
Wordless, I am screaming,
Dance, Mama, dance!

Meditations

Ida, The Manor of Northwest Detroit, 2010

She offers novels. Half an hour into this visit,
as she folds beneath the awkwardness of us,

long quiets between the movements of this brief dance
that tries to bring us closer. I wonder how

she looked at seventh grade, at ninth, at graduation,
and whether she sings—her voice at five years old

still echoes in each glimpse that filters
through the haze of decades. She offers tapes,

a tape player, to send recorded sermons;
but things like that will be temptations.

Years of study can't be stolen from rest-home night stands,
become shiny baubles for bored residents or staff.

TV doesn't work, can't cut the veil between us, interrupt
this journey from strangers back to daughter-mother.

Some visits we just watch each other,
slight curves of mouth to offer comfort,

arms too closed to hold,
hands too still to speak.

In the silence when she leaves,
I listen for the voice of God.

LABYRINTH II
Ida's alternate self speaks of 1961

When Ida calls me out this time for shelter, she
is curled, fetal on a bed at Riverside.
Rocking, weeping like a girl again,
a new vise wrench of pain within her,
Khaki's leer reverberating off the labyrinth walls.
His brogans echo up the stairs, stop.
She tucks herself into me, farther,

wraps me around her until we are one.
Khaki rasps apology for her throbbing cheek,
for the ache of bruise, pulls our locked arms
toward him in the dark. Tugs at us to open
as we clench, yanks harder as we hold, my arms
a fortress for her at her chest. His sweet becomes
angry grating, harsh demand in low tones meant
not to wake the children. *Oh, God. The children.*

I see them in her mind's eye, sleeping down the hall.
As Khaki tugs, I hold her silent, hold myself, a shield
to keep her safe, but she peeks out from me, watching
this man she loves harden to blows, then pause.
He checks the bruise, says once again his sorry
as though by words he can make the bloods recede,
stop their darkening.

There is a sound of tearing—soft cotton pajama leg
does not peel away. He cuts away last layers
of her modest cloth, drags us to the edge.   Begins.
I feel the sting of his sweat in that cut upon her thigh
I am certain even this man did not mean.
I rock her as he rocks, try to hide this violation,
but feel her peering out beyond me.
Something in her breaks.
Something spirals away.

RIVERSIDE

Khaki's brother Joseph

Boy had a bad case of the beentas.
Beenta California. Beenta Germany.
Beenta Saudi Arabia, Turkey, then settled down
in Air Force housing the size of nowhere
with two kids and a wife.
'Bout to sit around at that metal desk
fillin' forms, handlin' papers, ordering supplies,
and be happy.

Anyone listenin' coulda told you
this would not turn out a dream life.
Young man taking orders all day long,
gettin' pushed around by Uncle Sam
and all the other shined-up boots then
comin' home to Ida. Needin' to be treated
like a king. Needin' to feel important
after all that nothing all day every day.
Then Ida asking 'bout groceries and shoes
for that oldest girl.   And milk. And
what happened to the hot water, and
I'm sure Ida woulda asked him more'n that—
gal smart as a tick, you know.

Every sneered command he'd put up with
all day prob'ly settled on Ida's face
when he got home after holdin' back
and holdin' back, all day long
'til one day he swung right out and
clocked her. Back of his hand throbbing
like a hung-over head, Ida on the floor,
he snapped to quick, saw what he'd done.
She took off up the stairs,

threatnin' to call God, the police, her brothers,
but Khaki downstairs with the phone,
so he threw his brogans up the stairs
to make her stay outta his face.

Told me later he paced the floor for hours,
wondering what the hell, then
put the girls to bed, tiptoed in
to make amends with Ida, but
her not about apology,
turned in on herself, locked her arms
across her chest, turned her face
and would not let go. Khaki
never could handle bein' told no, either.
Wrestled her down, I hear,
and took him what was his.

CONVERSATIONS AT THE MANOR
Rosie, Detroit. 2012

Mother sits in the common room, her face
angled toward lap as though a world
tugs her head with hidden hands.
Say to yourself *Ida*. Make it mantra
down the hall before you enter.
She remembers *Ida,* Ms. Smith,
Sweetheart. If you are daughter, too,
say *Ida* like a promise kept and swallow
the breath you held for hours as you drove
in from Ohio in your straining Chevrolet,
lumbered in from too far distant to be
daily familiar for her eyes.
Do not say *Mother* as you speak.
Say, *Mommy*—she remembers you
six years old with summer conjuntivitis,
remembers you curled and weeping
when you could not play, holding
your eyes open for the balm of healing.
And on days she does not leave
her shared-room cot, kneel
to meet at her eye level, watch
a child's squint smile consume the empty,
the shoulder of elation lift the spread.
Even if she cannot say your name,
say, *Mommy.* Let it live in your up-close
and watch her answer. Kiss
the wilted cheek that glows there still,
forehead creased by years of wonder,
or the lip crusted from lack.
Hear her whisper, *Love you, too.*

Surrogates

Rosie, 2012

For truth's sake, Ida, I long still
to tell you I remember
your trapped-doe eyes as Khaki held
me from you, made you target
for his Air Force boots as you cowered,
want to say I was much too young,
a bow-legged spritz of girl
tucked behind his victory snicker,
failing to understand the jagged breach
opened deep within you, but to share these

broken, useless words would be cruelty
with no purpose while you, so frail,
eke your way through long term care,
one hand, one wheelchair revolution at a time.
He's gone three decades now, a wisp of smoke
blowing over desert spans, spectre on street corners
someplace where they're serving Bud on draft
into friction-clouded old glass steins,
while his goatee, combed, no longer graying,
points toward a memory littered
with brash encounters.

I want to tell you which came first—you,
fresh from psychiatric care, frightened
on the stair, or Zola with her strange lilt,
strangled Turkish words, who embraced
him and her daughter lovingly and fed us
(your girls) at arms length out of pity,
thinking what a pair we were,
shuffled into her house from
nowhere else to go but worth the extra rent,
sugar-daddy nights and smoke-filled
rooms saturated with jazz and ready loving.

But time lines snagged by second hands
serve no purpose in your semi-private room,
your endless days simply sitting, little left
to say to strangers' faces that surround you
every day. I sit beside you, woman
thinned to skin and bone, and wonder
should I tell you I once hugged Zola, too,
buried my face into her soft below, tried
to find you there, but never called her Mother.
She did not smell the same as you to my five-year-old
self, and no one can take that homing scent away,
smooth away the imprint long ago ingrained.

MEAL TIMES AT THE MANOR
Ida, Detroit, 2012

This man speaks no English
anymore. He speaks
thrown hamburger, cold potatoes,
This isn't what I asked for!
Hellfire and hateful,
angry at worlds.

Knows no names anymore.
Knows *You Black bitch!*
and *Hey, bitch!*
and *Come back here, bitch!*
as they rush around to please
but he won't be pleased
no matter what they do.

Vitriol spills from his open wounds
as we wonder what swinging club
beat compassion from him,
what injury he anoints
with bitter words, what deep scar
he debrides with caustic spill.

You turn your chair away,
tune the whole show out,
spend meal times with the walls.
You find a space to see yourself,
listen for porch songs at sundown,
beyond the drone of TVs
in the common room.

You give your back to men
who want to put you in your place.

VIGILS

Regina, Sinai Grace Hospital, 2014

At Mother's bedside, people come in like they know us. Same as when we sat with her in the Manor common room. Hover and hug. Hover and hug. Shake, hover and hug. Like we're familiar, but we don't know them. We are no longer the seven-year-old with skinny, rangy arms or the five-year-old who hid in corners. Hover and hug. Shoulders back, shake, hover, hug. Over thirty years lost between us. Our history an endless redirect—Alabama, Ohio, Alabama, L.A. To Riverside, then back to Ohio. To respite in Grandmother's arms. We'd like to do more than smile and nod, grasp loose, polite hands, hear strangers' surprise at how we've grown, our own children long ago adult. Hover and hug. Hover and hug. Shake, hover, hug. A family binding itself back together, the years between us all a long indictment. They were not there to save us from a children's hell. From the leather strap that scarred Rosie's leg for years. From weeks of hunger, as Khaki tried to father us. They waved goodbye as we were shuffled onto a bus. Weren't there as we were passed about and chased with knives. But this is not about us. This is thank God somebody comes to Mother's bedside. That all those years she's had these folks to love her. Hover and hug. Hover and hug. Shake, hover, hug. Look how they make her smile. They make this other Ida say, *I'm alright now.*

Sinai's Grace

Ida, August, 2014

My mind is awake and waiting
My tongue has a broken tip
As soon as I sleep, you wake me
Why won't you leave me alone?

My tongue has a broken tip
My whole body a sore
Why won't you leave me alone?
You talk over me like I'm not here

My whole body a sore
My bones press through to skin
You talk over me like I'm not here
You see only a body that's dying

My bones press through to skin
When you turn me to lie where no muscle
You see only a body that's dying
Put me back! is what I scream

When you turn me to lie where no muscle
My leg pulls away from my hip
Put me back! is what I scream
You leave as though I have said nothing

My leg pulls away from my hip
My dead right arm hangs exposed
You leave as though I have said nothing
The Young One comes for pressure, blood

My dead right arm hangs exposed
I protect the limp thing with my other
The Young One comes for pressure, blood
Pulls my body like she knows better

I protect the limp arm with my other
Use the left! Again I scream
Pulls my body like she knows better
She does not know anything

Use the left. Again I scream
What she won't understand she ignores
She does not know anything
It's as if I have no voice

What she won't understand she ignores
Your sing-song replies are insult
It's as if I have no voice
I am duty you have to fulfill

Your sing-song replies are insult
You treat me like I do not matter
I am duty you have to fulfill
You ignore me and speak to my daughter

My mind is awake and waiting
Only my tongue has a broken tip.

Back

Ida, Sinai Grace Hospital, Detroit, 2014

Back straight, eyes clear and open
I sit watching from the bed.
Three of them in white coats, talking.
To each other, to my daughters,
not even to both of them.
To the Manor manager, social worker,
nurse. Not to me. About me.
How frail I am, how damaged.
How they brought me back,
my stopped heart's practiced waking.
How they fear they'll break my bones
resuscitating what's left of me.
How they wish my children would decide
whether to risk such measures.
Why even try when this old pump stops again.
I am stunned, speechless, afraid
of seizures I can't remember,
stoppages I can't recall. Always.
White-coated pronouncements
as if I cannot hear. Their
white skins. Their near-white lies—
not to me. About me, I think
and hear my daughter tell them,
She is listening. Still they give
their backs to absent me,
withhold nothing, change nothing.
And I, held by this tongue again,
this knotted beast, this barrier between,
this crusted, wordless sloth
that holds me captive
while I watch, breathe,
Speak to me.   Ask.   Me.
Awake.
Here.
Listening.

Morning, IV Time

Ida, Sinai Grace Hospital, August, 2014

Sows muscling for trough space Autauga mornings
opened every eye still sleepin', announced
daylight had reached above horizon, while
high-pitched wails said Albie was out there
tippin' up feed buckets brimming
with corn cob, green stem, feeder grain
ready for the snout. Round-bodied snooze alarms,
singin' after the crow. Eldrina and I used to chase
piglets 'round that pen sometimes in summer.
Chasin' those little ones' frisky wiggle-tails.
More'n a time or two I slipped in all that muck,
messed up another pair o' cotton shorts
and got the switch, but not at mornin'.

Without lookin' we knew Daddy'd be
on his tractor, heading toward the front acres
where cotton, 'lope and melon waited
to be managed. He was good at that.
Easy to do, manage the life of things
that grow in stillness, things that move
so slow your eye can't see. Don't take speed
to catch a slow shell, though. You know
that old fable. Best to keep on movin' somehow.
All them fruit got ta do is wait for a wink
from Daddy's gray-rimmed eyes ta never
go to waste. 'Ventually they all go ripe, full
or full of seed and just 'bout ta bust—'bout the time
their skins can't hold life back another day.

I am familiar with the way of melons, how
they swell and sit, take up rain and wait,
drink that shimmer in through shallow roots

yielding just enough. Can almost smell 'em
strewn all over in the leaves. I bend to pick a treat,
then wake up, empty-handed in this strange Detroit
room, look around and, *Oh, I'm still here.*
I wait for The Nice One to come turn me over,
only this skin here can't keep the ripeness in.
Feels like these old bones been takin' back
'stead o' givin' out. I am the stem that's left
after Daddy walked the platte. Nothin'
'tween me and the wither but that
steady drip managed by practiced hands.

The Visitor

Sinai Grace Hospital, June, 2014

Goosebumps rise on my daughter's arm
when I try to tell her.
     Look. I say, *Look,*
and raise my eyes beyond the IV pole
to where I saw him.

This bastard tongue so clumsy. I repeat each word
so many times I've given up explaining.
I show her with my eyes,
when she asks, *What?*

I could tell her it is Mama, Daddy, friend
or angel come to take my hand,
Lord, or spectre—all of these she might believe
and hold me all the way to surrender.

She examines the light and me.
A ripple of clenched teeth in her cheek,
arms 'cross her belly. A slow, chin-raising swallow.
She steps back from my reaching face.

How do I show her what I see beyond this room,
past this bright light overhead, into a wide expanse
that leaves me unafraid?
     Look. I say with presence, *Look.*
She is earthbound, looks back into me
with searching, fearful eyes.

To a Sound of Water

Palliative care nurse, Detroit, 2014

She was fine
when I checked her

2:00 a.m.
just a little moan
when I turned her

A tiny bit of morphine

She was sleeping
quiet
just a little moan

then
this morning
gone

Choice

Ida, June, 2014

Full throttle from standing start
is how you go out
'less you don't want remembered.
None of this clinging to ledges, bent
fingers slipping on wind-blast,
long fall just enough to help
you linger.

Calloused hands
grip reminders
of all you once could do,
and how you love
or grab life's muscled arm
to pull it flat into your space,
peel its dimpled rind right open,
push its limits, goad it
to be, do, make, hold, whisper
but not quite break your normal
unless you say
Go, full throttle, standing.

Afterword

Imagine standing at the bedside of your mother, watching her be, in turn, condescended to or ignored by well-meaning medical staff over and over at a critical time in her life. Such an occurrence became the impetus for this manuscript. It seemed to me that her caregivers felt she had lost the ability to speak for herself, understand things for herself, make decisions for herself. As if she had become a job to her caregivers, another task to do, another body to tend among others on daily rounds, while the person in the bed had become invisible. My mother, who was awake and alert, listened to every word while her caregivers spoke as if she was not in the room. Seeing that became the catalyst for this collection.

Upon hearing some of these poems in live audience, many people have assumed this collection to be wholly biographical. It is not. I was estranged from my mother at an early age and cannot know what happened in the years between that estrangement and the point when we were reunited. All I know is watching how she was treated during that acute-care hospital stay made me aware of how we, as a society, treat the aging and the infirm. Each one has a story. Each one has met challenges or known victories. Each is a person whose life matters, a life we should not take for granted.

The Ida of this collection has endured a life interrupted by mental illness and its stigmas, multiple strokes, and the extended frailty introduced when one can no longer consume food normally. She'd been reduced to skin and bone beneath the clothes that hid her wasting body. Her mind was active and in no way diminished or affected, while she had been assumed to have dimentia. She was a passive woman, yet her life is still a life we should honor and respect. She was an "each one," and this book is an attempt to put the flesh back on her bones. It is a gesture of empathy that I hope will become contagious.

Perhaps at some point in our lives, we will meet an Ida. I pray we will each have opportunity to listen, to say "tell me your story," to offer an open heart and ear to someone who feels forgotten. Maybe in our final or most challenging days, someone will take time to notice and listen also to us.

About the Author

Rose M. Smith is a former software engineer and currently an IT analyst in Central Ohio. She has been called by fellow editors *a quiet visionary spanning the worlds of performance poetry and literary print, challenging and enriching the norms of both.* By fellow performers, *a shy, quiet atomic bomb* with the stunning ability to reveal the extraordinarily human in ordinary situations and characters. Rose is a Cave Canem fellow whose work has appeared in *Minola Review, Snapdragon, Main Street Rag, Third Wednesday, pluck!, The Examined Life, Kinfolks Quarterly, Naugatuck River Review, A Narrow Fellow,* and other journals, as well as multiple anthologies. She is author of *Shooting the Strays* (Pavement Saw Press, 2003), *A Woman You Know* (Pudding House Publications, 2005), and most recently *Holes in My Teeth* (Kattywompus Press, 2016). She was co-editor of *Cap City Poets, Columbus and Central Ohio's Best Known and Requested Poets* (Pudding House Publications, 2010). Rose is currently a senior editor for Pudding Magazine.

Glass Lyre Press

exceptional works to replenish the spirit

Glass Lyre Press is an independent literary publisher interested in technically accomplished, stylistically distinct, and original work. Glass Lyre seeks diverse writers that possess a dynamic aesthetic and an ability to emotionally and intellectually engage a wide audience of readers.

Glass Lyre's vision is to connect the world through language and art. We hope to expand the scope of poetry and short fiction for the general reader through exceptionally well-written books, which evoke emotion, provide insight, and resonate with the human spirit.

Poetry Collections
Poetry Chapbooks
Select Short & Flash Fiction
Anthologies

www.GlassLyrePress.com

www.ingramcontent.com/pod-product-compliance
Lightning Source LLC
Chambersburg PA
CBHW020126130526
44591CB00032B/543